Leader's Guide
for group study of

Be
Dynamic

Warren W.
Wiersbe

Leader's Guide prepared by
ERNEST SLATER

Eight Multiuse Transparency Masters (for visual aids) are included in a removable center section. Instructions for using the Multiuse Transparency Masters are on pages 5-6.

D1715320

VICTOR BOOKS®
A DIVISION OF SCRIPTURE PRESS PUBLICATIONS INC.
USA CANADA ENGLAND

ISBN: 0-89693-959-6

VICTOR BOOKS
A division of SP Publications, Inc.
Wheaton, Illinois 60187

Introduction

Be Dynamic is an able exposition of the first 12 chapters of the Acts of the Apostles. Dr. Wiersbe shows how the earliest chapters of church history are directly relevant to today's church. As you pursue this study you will soon realize that, though some remodeling has taken place, the church is essentially the same today as it was in the days of the apostles. The same dynamic found in the early church is still available to us today.

Along with *Be Dynamic* and this Leader's Guide, there are other resources that would be valuable in preparing for each session. The following are suggested:

General Reference:
   Strong's Exhaustive Concordance of the Bible. James Strong. Abingdon.
   Young's Analytical Concordance to the Bible. Robert Young. Thomas Nelson.
   Zondervan Pictorial Bible Dictionary. Edited by Merrill C. Tenney. Zondervan.
Commentaries:
   Commentary on the Book of Acts. F.F. Bruce. Eerdmans.
   The Acts of the Apostles. G. Campbell Morgan. Revell.
Special Subjects:
   Let the Bible Speak...About Tongues. Richard Schwab. Kregel.
   The Holy Spirit. John F. Walvoord. Zondervan.

May God bless and prosper this study as you prepare and as you share. Remember: Be studious, be prepared, be enthusiastic, be involved, be practical, be an example, and above all, be dynamic!

General Preparation

Before you tear into this leader's guide in all the excitement of preparing for session 1, take time to read pages 3-6.

If you are a little unsure of yourself because you're leading a group of adults for the first time, then follow the simple steps of FOCUS, DISCOVER, RESPOND outlined for each session.

FOCUS will arouse interest and focus your group's attention on the session topic. DISCOVER dynamically involves your group so that they can discover God's truth and its implications for their lives. RESPOND helps group members apply God's truth to their lives.

Even if you're a "veteran" adult group leader who has led multitudes in studies such as this before, this leader's guide can also help you. Simply skim the text for each session and choose the basic lesson parts that will aid you in your personal strategy.

Back to Basics

Read the entire text and this leader's guide. Underline important passages in the text and make notes as ideas come to you. Note any activities in the guide that take advance planning or preparation.

As leader, your enthusiasm for the subject and your personal interest in those you lead, will in large measure determine the interest and response of your group.

Plan to use teaching aids such as a chalkboard or an overhead projector during each session. If neither of these tools is available, use a magic marker on large sheets of newsprint.

Encourage group members to bring their Bibles to each session and use them. It is good to have several modern-speech translations on hand for purposes of comparison.

Getting Started Right

Start on time. This is especially important for the first session because it will set the pattern for the rest of the course.

Begin with prayer, asking the Holy Spirit to open hearts and minds and to give understanding so that the truth will be applied.

Involve everyone. Group involvement is a key to learning. As learners, we retain only 10% of what we hear, 20% of what we see, 65% of what we hear and see, BUT 90% of what we hear, see, and do.

Promote a relaxed environment. Arrange your chairs in a circle or semicircle. This promotes eye contact among members and encourages more dynamic discussion. Be relaxed in your own attitude and manner. As leader, address people by name to help others get acquainted.

Adapting the Course

This material is designed for quarterly use on a weekly basis, but it may be readily adapted to different uses. To use the course over a 12- to 13-week period, simply follow the lesson arrangement as it is given in this guide. Combine sessions if you have fewer weeks in which to cover the material. In some ways, this guide is like a smorgasbord of teaching ideas. As leader, *you* must pick and choose those activities in each session that will best satisfy the spiritual needs of your group members. You can't possibly expect them to digest it all!

A Final Word

Be motivated to master your subject so that you can be the kind of teacher Solomon describes in Ecclesiastes 12:10: *For the Preacher was not only a wise man, but a good teacher; he not only taught what he knew to the people, but taught them in an interesting manner (The Living Bible,* © 1971, Tyndale House Publishers).

MTM Instructions ────────────────────

"What's an MTM?" you ask. It's a Multiuse Transparency Master. Several MTMs are provided for you in the removable center section of this guide; MTMs are designed to increase your teaching impact.

The Victor Multiuse Transparency Masters in this guide will help you enliven your sessions and transmit vital information to the mind through the eye-gate, tying in with educators' recognition of the teaching value of visual aids. They are numbered consecutively (MTM-1—MTM-10) and show with what sessions they should be used. The guide gives specific directions for when and how to use each MTM in the lesson material.

Mechanics

Remove the center section of this guide by opening up the staples in the center. Lift the illustration sheets out and then close the staples again to keep the remaining portion of the guide together. To protect and flatten the MTMs, store them in a regular file folder.

Making Transparencies

You can make your own overhead transparencies inexpensively through the use of these transparency masters. This can be done in at least three ways:

1. *Thermal copier* (an infrared heat transfer process). This is probably the fastest way to make a transparency. Follow the instructions that come with the

copier equipment. Note that the color portions of the MTM are designed *not* to reproduce.

2. *Electrostatic process* (such as Xerox). Make sure that you use the correct film for the right machine. Some color on the MTM will come out gray. On certain MTMs some information, printed in a special light color, will *not* reproduce on machine-made transparencies. This gives you extra information to share orally or to fill in during the session.

3. *Trace your own MTM.* With minimum artistic ability, you can place a sheet of transparent film over the MTM and trace the major parts of the illustration. Exactness is not necessary. For best results, use clear 8½ x 11 sheets of polyester or mylar film (acetate works, but curls). By tracing your own transparencies, you add to your teaching options by being able to make overlays which can be used in a progressive, visually effective way.

Other Uses of Transparency Masters

1. *Visuals.* For small groups, use the MTMs just as they are, as printed visual aids. Or, if you put the MTMs inside clear "report covers," you can write on them.

2. *Spirit masters or mimeo stencils.* From these masters or stencils you can run off material for each group member. Both of these can be made on a 3M Thermofax copier.

Materials Resources

Check with an art supply store for materials such as fiber-tip transparency pens and polyester or mylar film sheets.

A number of distributors carry hundreds of products that can help to make your teaching more effective and fun—for you and your group. If an art store can't supply your needs, try one of these distributors:

Dick Blick Co., Box 1267, Galesburg, IL 61401 ● 309/343-6181; or 215/965-6051 (East Coast); or 702/451-7662 (West Coast).

Faith Venture Visuals, Inc., 510 East Main St., Lititz, PA 17543 ● 717/626-8503.

Nasco Arts & Crafts, 901 Janesville Ave., Fort Atkinson, WI 53538 ● 414/563-2446; or *Nasco West,* 1524 Princeton Ave., Modesto, CA 95352 ● 209/529-6957.

The Faith of the First Christians

TEXT, CHAPTER 1

A QUICK LOOK

Session Topic   Faith in the resurrected Christ is the dynamic of Christianity.

Session Goals   You will help group members:
1. Define the word *dynamic* as it relates to Acts 1–12 (*Focus*).
2. Relate the dynamic of the Resurrection to daily experience (*Discover*).
3. Apply the dynamic of Christ's resurrection in their lives (*Respond*).

GETTING READY

What You'll Need

Bible
Be Dynamic
Concordance
Dictionary
Overhead projector
Chalkboard and chalk
Paper and pencils

Getting Ready to Teach

1. Distribute copies of *Be Dynamic* to group members at least a week before your first session. Ask group members to read the first chapter of the text and the first chapter of Acts.
2. Read the Book of Acts in one sitting. Then reread the first 12 chapters several times. This will help you relate the specific details of each session to the overall development of Acts.

3. Read *Be Dynamic* through at least once. Underline points that stand out in your mind. Make notes of things that you wish to investigate. Then reread chapter one, making an outline of its contents.
4. Using the text and available reference materials (see the introduction to this Leader's Guide), prepare an introduction to the Book of Acts.
5. Using a concordance, study the key words of Acts: power, witness, one accord, prayer, kingdom, resurrection, raised, and risen.
6. Make two lists of verses in which you find the word *power* associated with the Resurrection. In one, list those verses which speak of God's power in the resurrection of Christ. In the second, list verses which speak of the power of Christ's resurrection in the Christian.
7. Using a dictionary, write out a concise definition of the word *dynamic*.

THE LESSON

FOCUS

1. If this is a new group, take time for introductions. Have each group member give their name and a little background about themselves. During the sessions use group members' names whenever possible.

2. Give an introduction to the Book of Acts, including its author, outline, theme, key verse, time frame, and key words.

3. Remind the group that the text you are using is *Be Dynamic*. Point out that the word *dynamic* comes from the Greek word *dunamis,* often translated "power." Read Acts 1:8 to illustrate. Explain that this Greek word is the root of such words as *dynamic, dynamite,* and *dynamo.* Relate your definition of the word *dynamic* to Acts 1:8. If time allows, ask someone to read Romans 1:16 and 1 Corinthians 1:18. Then relate your definition of dynamic to these verses.

DISCOVER

1. In his Preface, Dr. Wiersbe makes an important point about nonrepeatable events, transitional happenings, and basic spiritual principles. Illustrate this from Acts 1:15-26 (nonrepeatable event: selection of Matthias; transitional happening: casting of lots; basic spiritual principle: obedience to God's Word). Ask group members to offer other examples of these categories from chapter 1. Point out that there will not always be an equal number in each category.

2. Divide your group into five research teams, assigning to each one of the following passages: Matthew 28; Mark 16; Luke 24; John 20–21; and 1 Corinthians 15:3-7. Issue to each team paper and pencil and instruct them to list the proofs of Christ's resurrection found in the passage. Recall the teams after five minutes and ask them to report their findings. List proofs on the chalkboard. Share with the group your study of the word *power* in relation to Christ's resurrection.

3. Discuss Acts 1:8 in relation to the Resurrection. Ask: **What relationship is there between the receiving of the Holy Spirit and the Resurrection? Between being witnesses and the Resurrection?** Point out that the resurrection of Christ is a key element in every sermon in the Book of Acts.

4. Discuss how faith in the resurrected Christ affects our unity (Acts 1:12-14), our prayer lives (1:14, 24-25), and our knowledge of God's will (1:15-23). Relate Dr. Wiersbe's illustration of a thermometer and a thermostat to all three areas.

================= RESPOND =================

1. Explain how one can know Jesus Christ as personal Saviour. Then discuss with the group the difference between intellectual understanding of Christ's resurrection and faith in the resurrected Christ.

2. Ask group members to examine the quality of their faith. Is it a living faith in a living Lord? Point out that one element of life is growth. Are they growing in their relationship with believers, prayer, and God's Word? Another element of life is reproduction. Are they witnesses? Are they sharing the Living Christ with others?

================= ASSIGNMENT =================

1. Have group members read through the Book of Acts if they have not yet done so. Ask them to study Acts 2 and chapter 2 of the text.

2. Have group members keep a log entitled "Accidentals and Essentials." Ask them to divide the log into three categories: nonrepeatable events, transitional happenings, and basic spiritual principles. Ask them to record under the proper category the events of each chapter of Acts.

Power from Heaven!

TEXT, CHAPTER 2

A QUICK LOOK

Session Topic The Holy Spirit is the dynamic of the church's existence and effectiveness.

Session Goals You will help group members:
1. Visualize the reality of the church's existence (*Focus*).
2. Discover the relationship of the Holy Spirit to the church (*Discover*).
3. Realize that walking in the Spirit is essential to their witness (*Respond*).

GETTING READY

What You'll Need
Bible
Be Dynamic
MTM-1 and -2
Overhead projector
Chalkboard and chalk
Loaf of bread
Candles
Church constitution

Getting Ready to Teach
1. Purchase a loaf of unsliced bread, candles, and other birthday decorations. These will be used to remember the birth of the church. Make sure you have 19 candles (one for each century of the church's existence).
2. Continue your own log of "Accidentals and Essentials" (see *Assignment #2* from session 1). Under which category would you place these events: clo-

ven tongues like as of fire; the disciples being filled with the Holy Spirit; speaking with other tongues; and Peter's sermon? How would you categorize the early church's characteristics given in verses 41-47?

3. Study Acts 2 and chapter 2 of *Be Dynamic*. This session covers a great amount of material, some of which is the subject of much debate today (i.e., tongues, Spirit baptism, and baptismal regeneration). Therefore, this session can easily become a negative one, generating heat rather than light. Have your material well in hand. Guide the group into appreciation and appropriation of the truth that God the Holy Spirit dwells in them.

4. Study Dr. Wiersbe's three characteristics of a Spirit-filled church. These are located in chapter 5 of the text under the subtitle, "The Generosity of the Believers."

5. Prepare overhead transparencies of MTM-1 and MTM-2.

6. If your group is part of a church, use your church's constitution, particularly the statement of purpose or objective, in a comparison with the characteristics of the church of Acts 2.

THE LESSON _____

FOCUS

Display the loaf of bread with birthday candles and decorations before the group arrives. As you begin the session, light the candles and announce that a very special birthday is being remembered. Without inferring to the group whose birthday, lead them in singing "Happy Birthday." It should be interesting to see how many group members have caught on and supply the word church at the appropriate place in the song.

After singing, ask: **Why do you think a loaf of bread was used instead of a cake? Why one loaf rather than two? Why are there 19 candles? Why are lighted candles especially appropriate?**

DISCOVER

1. Write these words on the chalkboard: NONREPEATABLE EVENTS, TRANSITIONAL HAPPENINGS, and BASIC SPIRITUAL PRINCIPLES. Ask group members to share their conclusions from their logs of "Accidentals and Essentials." List their findings under each category and discuss.

2. Point out to the group that Acts 2 records the fulfillment of the

prophecy in Acts 1:5. You can demonstrate this point by comparing the various references to this prophecy:

☐ During Christ's ministry, Spirit baptism is spoken of as a future event. "He *shall* baptize you" (Matt. 3:11; Mark 1:8; Luke 3:16; John 1:33).

☐ At Christ's ascension, He still speaks of it as a future event. "Ye *shall* be baptized" (Acts 1:5).

☐ No further mention is made of this prophecy until Acts 11:15-17 when Peter defends his mission to the Gentiles by recounting John's prophecy and relating it to their experience at Pentecost. This is also in keeping with Christ's statement in Acts 1:5, "Not many days hence."

3. Explain that fire is typically used in Scripture as a sign of either God's pleasure or displeasure (Lev. 9:22-24; 10:1-2). But fire is also the sign or symbol of God's presence. Using MTM-1, lead the group in a study of God dwelling *with* His people in the Old Testament (Ex. 25:8); and in the New Testament, dwelling *in* His people (John 14:16-17, 23). Explain that Israel had seen God take up residence in the tabernacle in Moses' day and again in the temple in Solomon's day. In Acts, on the Day of Pentecost, Israel saw God take up residence in the believers. The tongues of fire were a sign to Israel that God had moved. Ask several group members to read 1 Corinthians 3:16-17; 6:19; 2 Corinthians 6:16; and Ephesians 2:19-22. Point out that the word translated "temple" does not refer to the building in general, but is the term used for the holy of holies—that part of the temple where God manifested His presence.

4. Point out to the group that Acts 2:38 seems to imply that sins are forgiven through baptism. Have someone read Acts 2:38. Then explain Dr. Wiersbe's point that the Greek word translated "for" in verse 38, probably means "on account of" or "on the basis of." Illustrate this by the following examples: "He was given a bonus for his good work." "He got a ticket for speeding." Obviously the good work and the speeding came first. Have someone read Matthew 3:1-9. Point out that John is baptizing people who *have* repented. Likewise, Peter is baptizing people whose sins have been remitted.

5. Read Acts 2:41-42 and ask group members to locate the primary characteristics of the first church (received the Word, baptized, apostles' doctrine, fellowship, breaking of bread, and prayer). List them on the chalkboard as they are located by the group. Then discuss each in relation to your own church. Read the purpose statement from your church's constitution and discuss it in relation to these characteristics. Discuss the responsibilities of Christians to the Holy Spirit.

6. Using MTM-2, explain the three characteristics of a Spirit-filled church. Emphasize that the Holy Spirit is responsible for these characteristics. Read and discuss with the group the Scripture verses under "At Pentecost" (Acts 2:44, 47).

RESPOND

Point out that the miraculous activity of the Holy Spirit in Acts 2 gained the attention of people in Jerusalem, but it was the daily activity of the Holy Spirit in the believers that sustained their attention. Read Acts 2:44-47 and point out that it was the *daily* Spirit-filled living of believers that prompted *daily* conversions (vv. 46-47). Encourage group members to maintain their relationships with each other, for the Holy Spirit indwells *all* believers. If we grieve a brother or sister, we also grieve the Holy Spirit and our witness is not dynamic.

ASSIGNMENT

1. Have group members read Acts 3:1–4:4 and chapter 3 of the text.

2. Have group members make a list of ways in which *name* is used in the sense of authority today. Give, "Stop in the name of the law" as an example.

3. Have group members continue logging the "Accidentals and Essentials" of the Book of Acts.

The Power of His Name

TEXT, CHAPTER 3

A QUICK LOOK

Session Topic   The authority of Jesus is the dynamic of Christian witness.

Session Goals   You will help group members:
1. Define their concept of authority (*Focus*).
2. Recognize the delegation of Jesus' authority in witnessing (*Discover*).
3. Examine the demeanor of their witnessing (*Respond*).

GETTING READY

What You'll Need
Bible
Be Dynamic
Concordance
Dictionary
MTM-3
Overhead projector
Chalkboard and chalk
A quarter

Getting Ready to Teach
1. Study chapter 3 of *Be Dynamic* and chapters 3 and 4 of Acts. Compare Peter's sermon in these chapters with his sermon in Acts 2. Note the similarities and differences.
2. Continue your log of "Accidentals and Essentials." This exercise is not only valuable in understanding the Book of Acts, it also demonstrates the application of a basic principle of interpretation that can be used with any biblical passage.

3. Prepare an overhead transparency of MTM-3.
4. Using your concordance, do a word study of *authority* and its related term, *name*. Remember that many times the English word *power* is used to translate the Greek word for authority as well as to translate *dunamis* (power).
5. Look up the words *authority, power,* and *sovereignty* in the dictionary. Prepare definitions for *Focus #2*.

THE LESSON

FOCUS

1. Introduce this session as follows: The main subject in this session is authority. The words *power* and *authority* are quite often used interchangeably, but there are differences. For instance, a policeman, by his authority, can stop a car by putting up his hand. Yet that same policeman cannot stop a car simply with his hand. Or a thief may have the power to carry a TV set out of a house, but that same thief does not have the authority to take the TV. Power connotes the idea of might; authority, the idea of right.

2. Share with the group your definitions of authority, power, and sovereignty.

3. Explain that the word *name* is often used in the sense of delegated authority. Ask group members to share their examples of using name in this sense.

DISCOVER

1. Review with the group their findings for their logs of "Accidentals and Essentials."

2. Discuss the difference between Jesus' authority and the apostles' authority. (Jesus had absolute authority.) Have several group members read Matthew 7:28-29; 8:5-13; Mark 2:1-12; Luke 4:31-36. Point out that Jesus spoke and acted with complete authority. The apostles always appealed to Jesus as their authority. Have several group members read Acts 2:38; 3:6, 16; 4:10, 12, 30; 8:12; 9:27-29; 16:16-18.

3. Using MTM-3, discuss the issue of God's sovereignty and man's free will. Read Acts 2:22-24, 36-39 and ask group members to identify God's sovereignty and man's free will as expressed in those verses. Explain that the principle of authority lies behind the issue of sovereignty and free will. The contest is as old as Genesis 3. Man either resists or submits to God's authority. Point out that God exercises His authority primarily to bless and save man.

15

4. Discuss the necessity of *both* repentance and conversion in salvation. Some teach that repentance is only for the Jews and it should not be included in presenting the Gospel. Acts 20:21 should be enough to counter that idea. Illustrate the unity of these two concepts by displaying a quarter. Showing each side in turn, ask: **Is this a quarter?** Describe the front of the quarter in detail. Then describe the back. Ask: **How can both sides be a quarter when they are entirely different?** (Because a quarter has two sides.) Point out that repentance and conversion, though different, are two sides to saving faith. Both are necessary. If one is absent, then saving faith is absent. Discuss the importance of this in witnessing.

5. Explain that the first few chapters of Acts cover only a few months, yet great numbers of people were saved during that short period of time. Acts 2:41 mentions 3,000 souls. This figure most likely includes women as well as men. In Acts 4:4 the number of men has grown to 5,000, with no mention of women or children. It is not unreasonable to estimate the size of the church to be around 10,000 believers, not counting those who left Jerusalem after Pentecost and returned to their homes (Acts 2:9-11). These numbers seem exaggerated to us who are used to seeing people trust Christ one or two at a time. Point out that this is a transitional period. Many who responded were coming from "Old Testament" faith to "New Testament" faith. Like Simeon, they too realized that Jesus is the Lord's Christ, the One for whom they had waited (Luke 2:25-26).

RESPOND

Apply the principle of authority to witnessing. Explain to the group that the demeanor of their witness is as important as the message. If we come across as "holier than thou" or judgmental, we will not be given a hearing. Point out that we need to come in Jesus' name. He is the Judge who calls us to repentance. He is the Saviour in whom we place our faith. Read Acts 3:6, 12, 16 to illustrate. Ask group members to examine their attitudes and demeanors in witnessing.

ASSIGNMENT

1. Have group members study chapter 4 of the text and Acts 4:5-31.
2. Have members continue their "Accidentals and Essentials" logs.
3. Ask for a volunteer to prepare a report on the Sadducees. Have him or her answer such questions as: Who were the Sadducees? What did they believe? Why were they particularly upset with Peter's preaching?
4. Ask for a volunteer to prepare a report on the title "Jesus Christ of Nazareth." Have him or her answer these questions: Where is Nazareth? Why was Nazareth attached to Jesus' name? What attitude did the Jews have toward Nazareth?

Persecution, Prayer, and Power

TEXT, CHAPTER 4

A QUICK LOOK

Session Topic   In the face of persecution, God gives the dynamic of courage.

Session Goals   You will help group members:
1. Become aware of the common fear of witnessing (*Focus*).
2. Discover principles that motivated and sustained the courage of the early believers (*Discover*).
3. Design a personal program to overcome the fear of witnessing (*Respond*).

GETTING READY

What
You'll Need

Bible
Be Dynamic
MTM-2
Overhead projector
Chalkboard and chalk
Paper and pencils

Getting Ready
to Teach

1. Study chapter 4 of the text and Acts 4:5-31.
2. Study John 11:47-54; 12:9-19; and Acts 4:16-21. Prepare a list of the similarities and differences between the two occasions.
3. Continue your log of the "Accidentals and Essentials" in the Book of Acts.
4. Check with your two group members who accepted assignments. Offer help if needed.
5. Prepare an overhead transparency of MTM-2.

THE LESSON

FOCUS

1. Before the session begins, list the following fears, without definitions, on the chalkboard: ACROPHOBIA (fear of heights), AGORAPHOBIA (fear of open spaces), AVIOPHOBIA (fear of flying), CLAUSTROPHOBIA (fear of confined spaces), ERGOPHOBIA (fear of work), LATROPHOBIA (fear of doctors), OTOPHOBIA (fear of opening one's eyes), SITOPHOBIA (fear of food), TRIDECAPHOBIA (fear of the number 13).

2. Begin the session by asking group members to offer definitions for each word on the chalkboard. (Supply the definitions yourself if necessary.) Explain that some of these fears are common, some seem humorous, but all are very real to those who are afflicted by them. Ask group members to share some of their fears. Say: **The most common phobia is not on this list.** Ask: **What do you think is the most often expressed fear?** (fear of speaking in public, speaking before a group) **What would you think is the most often expressed fear among Christians?** (the fear of witnessing) Discuss the reasons, then explain that this session will give principles to overcome our fear of witnessing.

DISCOVER

1. Review briefly your log of "Accidentals and Essentials."

2. Have the person who accepted the assignment on the Sadducees give his or her report. Allow for a few minutes of discussion and questions following the report.

3. Explain to the group that, in New Testament times, the High Priest was head of the Jewish political body (the Sanhedrin) as well as the religious system. Annas was appointed High Priest in A.D. 6. Somewhat later his son-in-law, Caiaphas, was also appointed High Priest. When Annas was not in office, he still remained in power unofficially. Annas and Caiaphas were both prominent in Christ's trial before the Sanhedrin (John 18). In Acts 4, they again show up together at the arrest of Peter and John. Point out to the group that the Sanhedrin would be fully aware of the disciples' association with Jesus. Read John 28:13-16 and point out that Peter and John would certainly have been known by Caiaphas. Discuss the implications of this.

4. Point out that the Chief Priests' dilemma in Acts 4:16 was not new to them. They faced this problem before in regard to the raising of Lazarus. Have two group members read Acts 4:16-21 and John 11:47-54; 12:9-19. Discuss the differences of the advice and actions of the council on the two occasions.

5. Have the person who accepted the assignment on "Jesus Christ of Nazareth" give his or her report. Allow for a few questions after the report.

Ask someone to read 1 Corinthians 1:18-29. Discuss with the group God's reasons for using humble and despised means to accomplish His work. Discuss the practical effect this should have on us by way of encouragement in our witness.

6. Explain that the reference, in Acts 4:13, to Peter and John being unlearned and ignorant, does not mean that they could not read or write. Rather it means that they had no formal religious training—they had not sat at the feet of a rabbi.

7. Divide the group into four research teams, assigning to each team one of the following subjects: the Holy Spirit, prayer, the Word of God, and companionship. Give each team paper and pencils and ask them to discover the ways in which their subject aided the believers in remaining steadfast in the face of persecution. Recall the teams after ten minutes and have them report their findings. Point out that these four elements are essential in motivation and maintaining courage. Do not discount companionship. Contrast Peter's courage in this situation with his cowardice at Christ's trial. Ask: **What effect do you think John's presence had on Peter? What effect did Peter's presence have on John?**

8. Using MTM-2, discuss the three characteristics of a Spirit-filled church. Read Acts 4:31-33 and emphasize these three characteristics in regard to persecution.

=========================== RESPOND ===========================

Ask group members to review their weekly schedule and prepare a list with two columns. In the first column, ask members to list every situation in which they have contact with unsaved people (e.g., home, work, shopping). In the second column, have members list the names or occupations of the people they meet in each situation.

Next instruct group members to mark those situations in which they have been "silent witnesses." Ask them to pray for awareness and boldness in witnessing this week. Tell them to be prepared to share their victories at the next session.

=========================== ASSIGNMENT ===========================

1. Have group members study chapter 5 of the text and Acts 4:32–5:16.

2. Encourage members to continue logging "Accidentals and Essentials" from Acts.

3. Ask for a volunteer to prepare a list of the principles of giving found in Acts 4:32–5:16. Ask the volunteer to correlate his or her list with the principles found in 2 Corinthians 8–9.

4. If you decide on the dramatization for next session's Focus, select your players and prepare a script. Don't forget to set practice times.

Beware of the Serpent!

TEXT, CHAPTER 5

A QUICK LOOK _____

Session Topic   The church maintains its purity through the dynamic of discipline.

Session Goals   You will help group members:
1. Be made aware of God's place in discipline (*Focus*).
2. Consider the process of discipline from God's viewpoint (*Discover*).
3. Discipline themselves in order to be pure before God (*Respond*).

GETTING READY _____

What You'll Need
Bible
Be Dynamic
MTM-2 and MTM-4
Overhead projector
Chalkboard and chalk

Getting Ready to Teach
1. Study Acts 4:32–5:16 and chapter 5 of the text.
2. Continue your log of "Accidentals and Essentials," giving special attention to principles of giving and discipline.
3. Remind your volunteer to be prepared for the report on the principles of giving in Acts 4:32–5:16. Offer help if needed.
4. Prepare an overhead transparency of MTM-2 and MTM-4.
5. If you choose the drama for the Focus, contact the members of your cast and arrange a rehearsal before the session.

THE LESSON

1. Have group members share the results of their prayers for boldness in witnessing. (See Respond, session 4.)

2. (*Option 1.*) Prepare a short dramatization of Ananias and Sapphira's sin. Ask for volunteers to play the parts of Peter, Ananias, Sapphira, and the two pallbearers. Your script would be taken from Acts 5:1-10. Feel free to make additions in order to make the dramatization as creative as possible. (*Option 2.*) Share the following anecdote.

> Michelangelo was one of the greatest artists in history. He is most widely known for his frescoes in the Sistine Chapel. But he preferred to be known as a sculptor. Some of his better known works of sculpture are *Moses, David,* and the *Pieta.* Many of his sculptures were commissioned to be placed in alcoves or niches in the walls of buildings. It was common for sculptors of that day in producing such works to finish only the front of the statue, since the back would never be seen. But not so with Michelangelo! Every sculpture was complete to the last detail. Asked why he took such pains when no one would ever see or appreciate his labor, Michelangelo replied, "God sees it!"

DISCOVER

1. Have the group share entries from their logs of "Accidentals and Essentials." Ask your volunteer to share his or her list of principles of giving. Explain that while the communal lifestyle of the early church followed basic spiritual principles, different systems can be employed to apply those principles. Ask group members to discuss how the common practices of giving follow spiritual principles.

2. Discuss the importance of proper motivation in giving. Ask: **What is the usual purpose served by giving someone a nickname?** (to call attention to a characteristic, i.e., Shorty) Explain that a surname is the same as a nickname. Ask: **Why does Luke make a special point of Joses' nickname?** (Acts 4:36) Ask: **In view of this, what do you think motivated Barnabas? What do you think motivated Ananias? Do you think Sapphira shared Ananias' motives? Does it matter if she did or not?**

3. Point out that Peter confronts Ananias and Sapphira publicly. Explain that the normal procedure in confrontation is first to confront the person or persons privately. Read Matthew 18:15-17. Ask: **Was Peter wrong in making this sin a public issue?** (No, their sin *was* public.) **How did their sin become public?** (Ananias made a public presentation of his gift, Acts 5:2; Sapphira lied publicly, Acts 5:8.) **How did Peter know that Ananias was lying about how much money he received for the sale of his property?** (God could have revealed it to Peter, but the sale of the property was a matter of public record.)

4. Using MTM-4, discuss the principle of God's severe judgments at the

beginning of a new period in salvation history. Discuss the possible reasons for differences in the three examples.

5. Point out that the hypocrisy of Ananias and Sapphira was doubly dangerous. It not only endangered their fellowship with Christ, but it also endangered the unity of the church. Their hypocritical offering would have fostered a spirit of competition and pride among the brethren. Remind the group that this is what happened at the church of Corinth. Ask three persons to read in turn: 1 Corinthians 1:10-13; 3:1-3; and 11:18-32. Underscore the fact that when God judged the Corinthians it was at the Lord's Table. Ask: **Why do you think God chose to judge them on that particular occasion? What does the Lord's Table proclaim about our relation to each other? Why would their hypocrisy at the Lord's Table be especially repugnant?**

6. Dr. Wiersbe rightly notes that what is described in this chapter is not a case of church discipline. However, it is discipline, and there are principles of discipline that can be applied to ourselves and our churches today. Ask the group to locate principles of discipline. List them on the chalkboard and discuss their application for today's church.

7. Using MTM-2, review the three characteristics of a Spirit-filled church. Emphasize the need of purification and maintaining purity in the church.

RESPOND

Using MTM-4, remind the group of the severity of God's judgments in each of these situations. Help your group see that even though God seldom judges sin in this fashion, He still abhors sin in His people. Explain that Ananias is an example of the tragic effects of sin in the life of an individual and in the lives of other believers. Read 1 Corinthians 11:31 and point out that self-discipline is the best discipline. Ask group members to bow their heads and quietly search their hearts and confess their sins to God, cleansing themselves from hypocrisy.

ASSIGNMENT

1. Ask group members to study chapter 6 of the text and Acts 5:17-42. Ask them to make a list of consequences of truth or truthfulness.

2. Ask for a volunteer to prepare a report on opposition to the truth in the Book of Acts. Tell him or her to trace the actions of the Jewish leaders in opposing the Gospel.

Truth and Consequences

TEXT, CHAPTER 6

A QUICK LOOK

Session Topic   Truth is the dynamic of persistence in witnessing.

Session Goals   You will help group members:
1. Recognize that truth has consequences (*Focus*).
2. Contrast the consequences of truth with the consequences of falsehood (*Discover*).
3. Resolve to witness, regardless of the consequences (*Respond*).

GETTING READY

*What
You'll Need*
Bible
Be Dynamic
Concordance
MTM-5
Overhead projector
Chalkboard and chalk

*Getting Ready
to Teach*
1. Study Acts 5:17-42 and chapter 6 of the text. Note statements which summarize a point. Look for ways to use them in developing the lesson. In particular use statements or illustrations from the text to develop the outline of MTM-5.
2. Using a concordance, prepare a study of the word *truth*. Use your findings in developing the lesson.
3. Prepare a transparency of MTM-5 and make copies to distribute to your group.
4. Check with the group member who volunteered to report on opposition to the truth in the Book of Acts. Offer help if needed.

THE LESSON _____

Relate the following story to the group:

    Some years ago this question was posed to several different people: "Could you tell the absolute truth for 24 hours?" Here are some of their replies to that question:

      "I don't think so. It would surely end up being embarrassing. Little white lies save a lot of grief."

      "If it was important I could. I'm very candid, and I know I occasionally hurt someone with frankness. I try hard not to be hypocritical, and of course, that doesn't always win friends."

      "Yes, if I knew I had to. But little lies are OK under certain circumstances, like when my boss asked how I liked my work."

      "No, this would be an intolerable world if everyone always told everyone else the truth. There is an element of cruelty in always being truthful."

    Ask: **What common themes run through these replies?** (lying is justifiable, truth has consequences) Point out that these are two sides of the same coin. We sometimes lie because we are afraid of the consequences of the truth. Reread the replies, asking your group to identify the stated or implied consequences.

    1. Point out that Dr. Wiersbe hints at the fact that in spite of the severity of the circumstances, this trial has its humorous moments. Ask your group to offer examples. (Here are the Sadducees who deny that there are angels. So what does God do? He sends an angel to deliver the apostles! Here is this body of judges who, having brought the apostles to trial, suddenly find themselves being tried by the defendants! Here is Gamaliel, a doctor of the law, a man of great reputation. But with all his knowledge and ability in the finest points of the law, he fails to render a decision!)

    2. Distribute copies of MTM-5 to group members. Discuss with the group the eight contrasts point by point. Use the following seed thoughts to help develop each point.

    □ *Sanhedrin.* (1) Envy, not truth, motivated them. They were not even honest with themselves. (2) They put the apostles in prison, a classic illustration of suppressing the truth in unrighteousness. (See Rom. 1:18.) (3) They doubted—Dr. Wiersbe uses bewildered; perplexed is good too. (4) Fear caused them to act in secret. (See John 3:19-21.) (5) When Pilate washed his hands before these same men, he said, "I am innocent of the blood of this just person; see ye to it." These men replied, "His blood be on us, and on our children." They said they accepted the responsibility of Christ's death. But when the apostles laid this responsibility at their feet, they refused to accept it! (See Matt. 27:20-26.) (6) They were "cut to the

They were all filled
with the HOLY SPIRIT

(Acts 2:4).

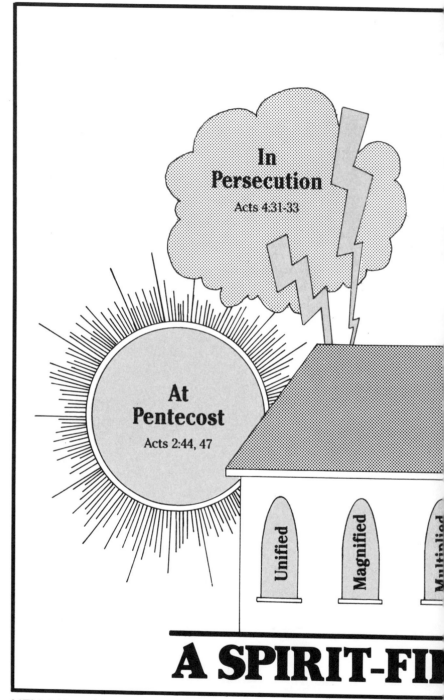

And now, brethren, I wot that through ignorance ye did it, as did also your rulers.

But those things, which God before had showed by the mouth of all his prophets, that Christ should suffer, he hath so fulfilled.

Repent ye therefore, and be converted, that your sins may be blotted out,

When the times of refreshing shall come from the presence of the Lord; and he shall send Jesus Christ, which before was preached unto you: whom the heaven must received until the times of restitution of all things, which God hath spoken by the mouth of all his holy prophets since the world began.

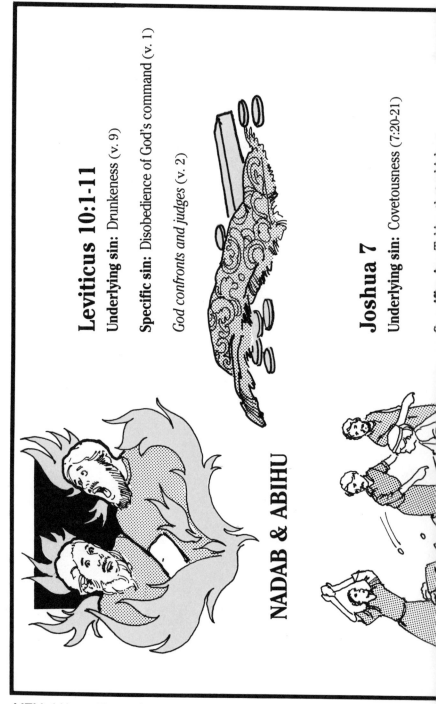

Leviticus 10:1-11

Underlying sin: Drunkenness (v. 9)

Specific sin: Disobedience of God's command (v. 1)

God confronts and judges (v. 2)

NADAB & ABIHU

Joshua 7

Underlying sin: Covetousness (7:20-21)

... of actions (v. 41)

6. Had clear conscience (v. 41)

7. Men of conviction (v. 29)

8. Peaceable (v. 31)

... consequences of actions (v. 28)

6. Had guilty conscience (v. 33)

7. Without convictions (vv. 38-39)

8. Violent (vv. 33, 40)

a field being prepared for seed.

PAUL SIMON

ROGRESS

Baptized Cornelius (Acts 10:48)

Accepted Cornelius as Equal (Acts 10:25-29)

Lodged Gentile Delegation (Acts 10:23)

Vision of Clean and Unclean Animals (Acts 10:10-16)

es with a Tanner (Acts 9:43)

ad Body (Acts 9:40)

(Acts 8:17)

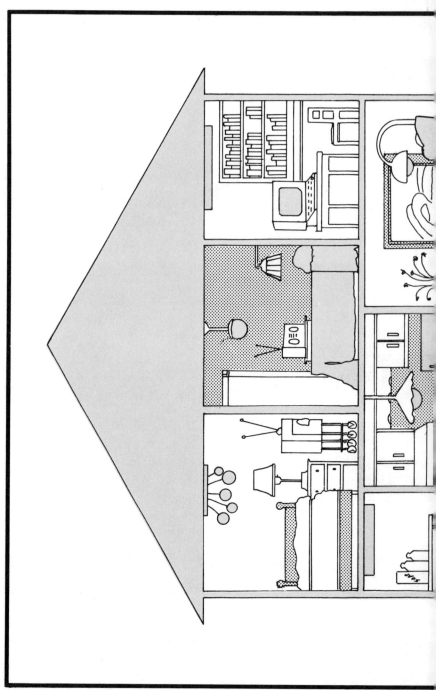

MTM-8 Use with session 12 of *Be Dynamic.*

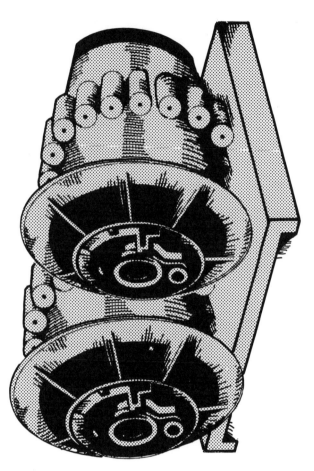

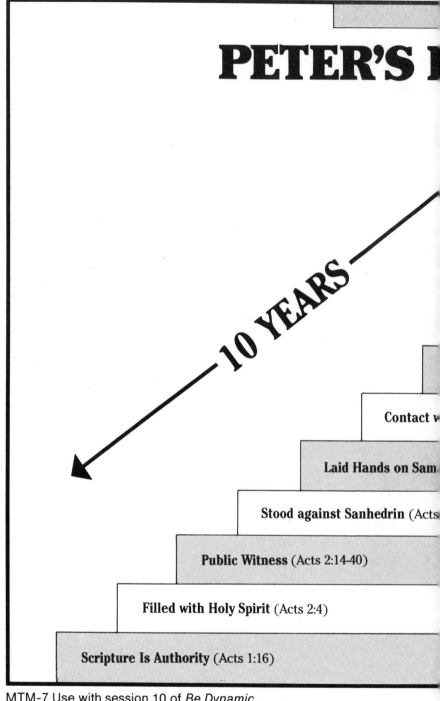

PETER'S I

10 YEARS

Contact v

Laid Hands on Sam

Stood against Sanhedrin (Acts

Public Witness (Acts 2:14-40)

Filled with Holy Spirit (Acts 2:4)

Scripture Is Authority (Acts 1:16)

MTM-7 Use with session 10 of *Be Dynamic.*

SAMARIA.

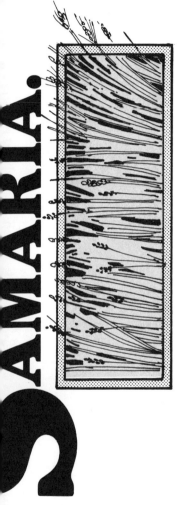

EUNUCH

a fruitful vine.

Error Contrasted with Truth

Acts 5:12-42

SANHEDRIN	APOSTLES
1. Dishonest (vv. 17, 28)	1. Honest (v. 30)
2. Suppressed truth (v. 18)	2. Declared truth (vv. 20, 42)
3. Uncertain (v. 24)	3. Certain (v. 32)
4. Hid behind closed doors (vv. 26-27)	4. Public—nothing to hide (v. 25)

MTM-5 Use with session 6 of *Be Dynamic*.

God confronts and Joshua judges (7:16-18, 24-26)

ACHAN

Acts 5:1-11

Underlying sin: Envy

Specific sin: Lying to God (vv. 3, 8-9)

Peter confronts and God judges (vv. 3-5, 8-9)

ANANIAS & SAPPHIRA

ACTS 3:13-21

Divine Sovereignty   Human Responsibility

The God of Abraham, and of Isaac, and of Jacob, the God of our fathers, hath glorified his Son Jesus;

Whom ye delivered up, and denied him in the presence of Pilate, when he was determined to let him go. But ye denied the Holy One and the Just, and desired a murderer to be granted unto you; and killed the Prince of Life,

Whom God hath raised from the dead; whereof we are witnesses. And his name, through faith in his name, hath made this man strong, whom ye

**After
Purifying**

Acts 5:12-14

**After
Problem-Solving**

Acts 6:5-8

ED CHURCH

The glory of the Lord filled the tabernacle (Exodus 40:34).

The glory of
the Lord filled the
house of Go

heart" (literally, "sawed through"). The Holy Spirit quickened their dead consciences. (7) Truth to them was relative and pragmatic. (8) They beat the apostles—the ultimate expression of falsehood. Satan is a liar *and* a murderer.

☐ *Apostles.* (1) "When ye slew" is blunt and direct. The truth is not hidden in theological jargon or misdirected tact but sharp as a sword. (See Acts 2:23; 3:14-15; 4:10.) (2) They spoke "the words of this life" and preached Jesus Christ. (See John 14:6.) (3) "We are His witnesses" expresses a calmness of soul, an unruffled spirit. They retained their composure because they knew where they stood—in the truth. (4) They were standing in the temple, not whispering in a corner. What a change from John 20:19. (5) They not only were willing to *bear* the consequences, they *rejoiced* in them. (6) They were shamefully treated but they were not ashamed. (See Matt. 5:11-12; Luke 6:22-23.) (7) Truth to them was absolute; it was not negotiable. (8) They preached forgiveness of sins to their persecutors. (See Romans 12:14, 17-21.)

Ask your group to share other consequences they may have found in their study.

3. Remind your group that opposition to the truth did not come from the criminal element, but from the religious element. Ask your volunteer to share his or her findings regarding the opposition to the truth in Acts. Discuss the implications of this.

===================================== RESPOND =====================================

1. Ask several volunteers to read aloud John 15:18-22; 16:1-3 and 2 Timothy 3:10-13. Point out that the severe consequences of standing for the truth cannot be avoided in an evil world. Truth is *never* popular, especially the truth of the Gospel.

2. Remind your group of their assignments to review their weekly schedules (Respond, session 4). Ask them to reaffirm their commitments to witness and rejoice in the consequences of it.

===================================== ASSIGNMENT =====================================

1. Ask group members to study Acts 6–7 and chapter 7 of the text.

2. Ask group members to find out the meaning of their first names. Ask them to think how their names have affected them. Ask them to think about whether or not they are happy with their names and why.

3. Ask a volunteer to prepare a brief report on Exodus 18 as it relates to delegating responsibility.

4. Ask a volunteer to prepare a brief study on the practice of "laying on hands" mentioned in Acts 6:6. Give the volunteer the following list of references: Numbers 27:15-23; Deuteronomy 34:9; Acts 8:14-19; 9:12-18; 13:1-3; 1 Timothy 4:14; 5:22.

Stephen, the Man God Crowned

TEXT, CHAPTER 7

A QUICK LOOK

Session Topic   Faithfulness is the dynamic of a victorious Christian life.

Session Goals   You will help group members:
1. Explore the significance of names in regard to character (*Focus*).
2. Observe the principle of faithfulness through the life of Stephen (*Discover*).
3. Practice the principle of faithfulness (*Respond*).

GETTING READY

What You'll Need
Bible
Be Dynamic
Concordance
MTM-2
Overhead projector
Chalkboard and chalk
Paper and pencils
3 x 5 cards

Getting Ready to Teach
1. Study chapter 7 of *Be Dynamic* and Acts 6–7.
2. Update your log of "Accidentals and Essentials."
3. Using a concordance, study the concepts of *stewardship* and *faithfulness* as they relate to each other.
4. Check with the two group members who volunteered to give reports. Offer help if needed.
5. Contact any elderly members and widows in your church congregation and make a list of their needs

(e.g., lawn mowing, shoveling walks, to be taken shopping, etc.). Be sure these are specific. Write each need on a 3 x 5 card, including the name, address, and telephone number of the person. Have these cards ready for the Respond section.

THE LESSON

FOCUS

Begin by pointing out that, as seen in session 3, a name involves authority. But a name also identifies. And a name also reveals and/or forms character. Relate the following anecdote.

Tommy, *never* Thomas or even Tom, was a frail "mama's boy." Growing up he very seldom played with the fellows, preferring rather to be with the girls. He would run home when games got rough. He became increasingly insecure and angry. At the age of 24 he had to leave college because he suffered severe indigestion and headaches. He proposed marriage but was refused. He finally decided he'd had enough. He grew sideburns and bought a new wardrobe. He also dropped the name "Tommy" and took his middle name. From that point on he was known as Woodrow—Woodrow Wilson.

Discuss this aspect of names. Ask: **How do you think your name has affected you?** Discuss the meaning of names, asking group members to share the meanings of their names. Relate this to Stephen.

DISCOVER

1. Review with the group your log of "Accidentals and Essentials."

2. Dr. Wiersbe notes three opportunities afforded by problems. Ask group members to locate them in the text. List each on the chalkboard. Briefly outline the problem in Acts 6:1-6. Then divide the group into three research teams and give each team paper and pencil. Have Team 1 list the factors that created the problem and the changes that were recommended to solve the problem. Have Team 2 list ways through which the believers exercised faith in each other. Have Team 3 list the ways in which the believers expressed love to one another. Recall the teams after 5 minutes to share their findings with the group.

3. List on the chalkboard the three qualifications given for the selection of the seven men. Discuss the importance of each qualification. Ask: **Why was honesty important? Why was wisdom important? Since this basically involved dividing up the food equally, what was the importance of the qualification of Spirit-filled? What are the dangers of placing people who are not spiritually minded in places of responsibility?**

4. Ask the volunteer who prepared the report on Exodus 18 to share his or her findings. Discuss the necessity and the benefits of delegating responsibility. Don't forget to note the benefits to the delegate.

5. Ask the volunteer who prepared a study of "laying on hands" to share his or her report. As you discuss the significance of this custom, ask group members to relate any occasions that they have witnessed this practice. Ask them to give their understandings and impressions of what they saw. Allow time for several responses and then discuss the topic with the whole group.

6. Using MTM-2, review the characteristics of the Spirit-filled church. Emphasize the effect that "Problem Solving" had in forming the Spirit-filled church.

7. Share the results of your study of *stewardship* and *faithfulness,* relating these concepts to the account of Stephen. Explain that stewardship and responsibility are interchangeable terms.

Ask group members to locate five characteristics displayed by Stephen in Acts 6:3-10. (honest report, v. 3; full of the Holy Spirit, vv. 3, 5, 10; full of wisdom, vv. 3, 10; full of faith, vv. 5, 8; full of power, v. 8) List these on the chalkboard as they are located by the group. Ask: **What idea is conveyed by the term *full*?** (That he was spiritual, wise, faithful, powerful. He was already a good steward.) **How did he arrive at this level of character?** (By accepting responsibility and growing thereby.) **In view of his maturity level, would you see Stephen as being overqualified to wait on tables? What character trait is implied in Stephen's willingness to accept this task?** (Humility)

Read Luke 16:10 and help your group see how this principle worked in the life of Stephen. Starting at the bottom of the chalkboard, list these phrases in the form of ascending steps (as shown):

Glorifying God in his death, 7:55-60.
Confronting the Sanhedrin, 6:12–7:54.
Debating with rabbis in the synagogues, 6:9-10.
Preaching among the people, 6:8.
Serving the believers, 6:5-6.

Point out that our word *martyr* comes from the Greek word for witness. Stephen was first of all a witness, a faithful witness. It was his *life* that gave meaning to his death.

========================= RESPOND =========================

Reread Luke 16:10. Remind your group that Stephen's coronation was the end result of a series of faithful responses to God. He did not despise any opportunity. No task was beneath him. As he took the opportunities, the opportunities grew, and he grew.

Explain to the group that you have collected some opportunities for service through which they can begin to follow Stephen's example. Share the needs you have written on the 3 x 5 cards and ask group members to volunteer to take one.

1. Have group members study chapter 8 of the text and Acts 8.

2. Have group members continue their logs of "Accidentals and Essentials."

3. Ask someone to prepare a report on the similarities between Simon's experience in Acts 8:9-24 and the experience recorded in John 6:24-71 (especially vv. 26, 60-71).

A Church on the Move

TEXT, CHAPTER 8

A QUICK LOOK _____

Session Topic   Like a seed, the Gospel is the dynamic of life, wherever it is sown.

Session Goals   You will help group members:
1. Be made aware of the satisfaction of sowing the seed of the Gospel (*Focus*).
2. Explore the ways and means of sowing the Gospel (*Discover*).
3. Renew their efforts in sowing the Gospel (*Respond*).

GETTING READY _____

What You'll Need
Bible
Be Dynamic
MTM-6
Overhead projector
Chalkboard and chalk
3 X 5 cards

Getting Ready to Teach
1. Study chapter 8 of *Be Dynamic,* highlighting the author's main points. Then read through Acts 8 several times.
2. Continue your log of the "Accidentals and Essentials" in the Book of Acts.
3. Prepare an overhead transparency of MTM-6.
4. Contact the group member who volunteered to give a report. Offer help if needed.
5. Prepare the assignment card (*Assignment #3*) for next session's volunteer report.

THE LESSON

FOCUS

1. Open the session with prayer. Then ask group members to think about how they became Christians. Ask: **How was the Gospel sown in your life?** Allow time for several group members to answer this question. If the group seems reticent, begin by discussing your own experience.
2. Discuss with the group the metaphor of sowing the seed of the Gospel. Ask: **In what ways is spreading the Gospel like sowing seed? In what ways can you participate in sowing the Gospel?**

DISCOVER

1. Review findings in your log of "Accidentals and Essentials."
2. Dr. Wiersbe explains the history of the Samaritans. Explain that the reason Assyria deported and imported peoples was to weaken the threat of organized rebellion in the countries they conquered. It was a very effective means of maintaining control over vanquished peoples. Discuss how this policy would work.
3. Some feel that Simon was a genuine, but carnal, Christian. The most serious objection to Dr. Wiersbe's view is the statement "Simon himself believed also," and added to this, Philip baptized him (v. 13). Help group members see that Simon's experience is basically the same as that found in John 6. Have your volunteer share his or her report comparing John 6:24-71 and Acts 8:9-24. Discuss the problem of "possessors" and "professors." To amplify this point, ask a group member to read Matthew 13:24-30, 36-43.
4. Dr. Wiersbe makes the very important point of Peter's use of the keys of the kingdom. Ask someone to read Matthew 16:13-20. Explain that Peter was told *not* to tell that Jesus was the Christ at that time. Peter's first proclamation was at Pentecost. Review Peter's role in Acts 2. Point out that although the 120 disciples were proclaiming "the wonderful works of God" (2:11), it was Peter who preached that Jesus was the Christ (2:36). On this occasion the Jews became the first members in the body of Christ. Point out that in Acts 8 even though the Samaritans had already believed in Jesus (8:12), it was not until Peter came and laid hands on them that the Samaritans became members of the body of Christ. Review the practice of laying on of hands. Discuss its significance in regard to the acceptance of the Samaritans into the body of Christ. Ask someone to read John 4:19-24. Point out the repetition of the words *we* and *you*. Then draw attention to Dr. Wiersbe's remarks on God not wanting two churches.
5. Discuss the importance of baptism in the Christian's life. Point out that believers regularly identified themselves with Christ through this public ritual. Help group members see the connection between a public confes-

sion of Christ and a consistent public witness for Christ. Point out the inconsistency of being a secret believer or a silent witness.

6. List on the chalkboard three means that God uses in sowing the Gospel.

☐ *God uses circumstances.* Ask: **What circumstances did God use in Acts 8?** (persecution) **What other circumstances might God use in our lives?** (job change, hospitalization, etc.) Amplify this point by showing how God used Paul's imprisonment in Philippi to reach the jailer.

☐ *God uses special leading.* Review Dr. Wiersbe's experience of God's leading and ask group members to share any experiences they have had.

☐ *God uses the normal routine of life.* Point out that the Samaritans and the eunuch continued in their regular activities. But in those activities, they were now witnesses for Christ. To illustrate this further, have someone read Mark 5:1-19, emphasizing verse 19. Point out that this kind of witness is the most common *and* often the most difficult.

7. Using MTM-6 discuss the relationship between seed and soil. Read Hebrews 4:2 and note that "the Word" is the good seed, and "faith" is the good soil. Both are necessary for the fruit of salvation. Discuss Saul's extreme agitation in Acts 8:3 and 9:1. Explain that this was evidence that the Spirit of God was preparing Saul's soul to receive the seed of the Gospel. Discuss the necessity of preparing the ground before planting.

RESPOND

1. Review the place baptism has in a Christian's life. Some group members may not have publicly identified themselves with Christ. Encourage them to do so.

2. Remind your group that the most common means of sowing the Gospel is in the daily routine of our lives. Ask group members to review their lists of situations where they have been silent witnesses. Encourage them to be good seed and sow themselves for Christ.

ASSIGNMENT

1. Have group members study chapter 9 of *Be Dynamic* and Acts 9:1-31; 22:1-21; 26:1-20.

2. Have members continue their logs of "Accidentals and Essentials."

3. Assign someone to do research on the subject: God's Goads. Have prepared a 3 x 5 card with the following information: (1) Define a goad (something that pricks). (2) How is the term used in Acts 26:14? (3) The goads (pricks) are not described, but two possibilities are: Christian witness (Acts 6:9-10; 6:15–8:3); and the Law (Romans 7:7-13). Explain how these acted as goads. (4) Are there other possibilities?

God Arrests Saul

TEXT, CHAPTER 9

A QUICK LOOK

Session Topic   Saul is an illustration of the dynamic of a purposeful life.

Session Goals   You will help group members:
1. Understand the idea of a life purpose statement (*Focus*).
2. Investigate the effects of a life purpose statement in Saul's conversion (*Discover*).
3. Formulate their own life purpose statement (*Respond*).

GETTING READY

What You'll Need

Bible
Be Dynamic
Concordance
Chalkboard and chalk
3″ x 5″ cards and pencils
Copies of your harmony of Acts 9:1-19; 22:1-21; and 26:1-20

Getting Ready to Teach

1. Study chapter 9 of *Be Dynamic* and Acts 9:1-31.
2. Continue your log of "Accidentals and Essentials."
3. Study the three records of Saul's conversion: Acts 9:1-19; 22:1-21; 26:1-20. Correlate the information and write a harmony of Saul's conversion. If possible, make a copy for each person in your group to follow in the session.
4. Using a concordance, study the phrase "Son of God."

5. Check with the person who accepted the assignment on "God's Goads." Offer help if needed. Be sure to prepare this assignment yourself.

THE LESSON

=========================== FOCUS ===========================

Explain to your group that one of the first things a person learns in composition class is to formulate a purpose statement, concisely giving the reason for the composition. Every composition, every speech, every lesson, and every sermon ought to have a stated purpose. So too should every life, especially a Christian's.

Read Joshua 24:15 and point out Joshua's purpose statement. Then have several group members read Galatians 6:14; Philippians 1:18-21; 3:8-14. Explain that Saul, called Paul, stated in no uncertain terms, his purpose in life. Point out that Paul's surrender to God still speaks today. His life and influence echoes down through the centuries and reechoes throughout the world today.

=========================== DISCOVER ===========================

1. Review with the group your log of "Accidentals and Essentials."

2. Discuss Jesus' approach to Saul in verse 4. Ask: **Why did Jesus call him by name twice?** (God does this at critical times in a person's life; e.g., Gen. 22:11; Ex. 3:4; 1 Sam. 3:10; Luke 22:31.) **Why did Jesus ask a question?** (To make Saul conscious of what he was doing, e.g., Gen. 3:9.) Draw attention to the fact that Jesus asked why Saul persecuted *Him*. Ask: **Why didn't Jesus say, "Why are you persecuting believers?" What two principles are implied in this form?** (All sin is sin against God, e.g., Gen. 39:7-9; and Christ is in the believer, e.g., John 17:22-23.)

3. Ask your volunteer to give his or her report on "God's Goads." Be sure the significance of Acts 6:9-10 is not overlooked. It probably was the synagogue which Saul attended (see chapter 7 of the text). Ask: **What effect might the events in Acts 6:10 have had on Saul?** In regard to Romans 7, ask: **What did the commandment, "Thou shalt not covet," have to do with Saul's actions at this time?** Discuss the place of these two "goads" in our lives today.

4. List on the chalkboard the two questions of Saul: WHO ARE YOU, LORD? LORD, WHAT WOULD YOU HAVE ME DO? Point out that these are the two basic questions of Christianity. The first implies salvation; the second, sanctification. Point out that the second question addresses the issue of life purpose. Discuss the application to finding God's purpose for life.

5. Dr. Wiersbe notes six different names for Christians in this section.

Ask group members to locate them in the text. List them on the chalkboard along with references. Discuss each in turn. Ask the group to think of ways in which each of these names relate to life purpose. Review the effect of names as discussed in the Focus section of session 7. Ask: **How does each of these names affect our attitudes as Christians?**

6. In discussing the place of Ananias in God's program, ask: **What possible reasons could be given for Ananias' selection? Why do you think God used Ananias rather than one of the apostles? What would the name Ananias mean to Saul?** (God is gracious, see chapter 5 of the text. Amplify this point with a brief examination of the word *grace* in Paul's letters.) **What is the significance of Ananias' address, "Brother Saul"?** (He accepted Saul as a fellow believer. It conveyed to Saul the principle of the unity of believers, an absence of hierarchy.) **What are some possible purposes of God in Ananias' life?**

7. Dr. Wiersbe observed four lessons to be learned from God's use of Ananias. Ask group members to locate them. List each on the chalkboard and discuss its relation to life purpose.

8. Point out that Saul immediately preached Jesus as the Son of God (v. 20). Explain that the phrase, "Son of God" is a messianic title. Share the results of your study with the group.

9. Dr. Wiersbe points out that between Saul's conversion and his appearance at Jerusalem at least three years had elapsed. During this time he was personally instructed by Jesus Christ. Discuss some possible reasons for this unique treatment. Explain that one plausible reason is that Saul was not only an apostle, but also a prophet. His message was like that of other prophets in that it was directly from God. Remind your group that Paul authored 13 of the 27 books in the New Testament.

══════════════ RESPOND ══════════════

1. Ask: **Why are Christians often without purpose?**

2. Review the idea of a life purpose statement. Then distribute 3 x 5 cards and pencils. Ask group members to formulate a life purpose statement. Ask them to take their statements home and refine them through the coming week. Announce that at the beginning of next session, opportunity will be given to share life purpose statements.

══════════════ ASSIGNMENT ══════════════

1. Have group members study chapter 10 of *Be Dynamic* and Acts 9:32–10:48.

2. Have group members continue their logs of "Accidentals and Essentials."

Peter's Miracle Ministry

TEXT, CHAPTER 10

A QUICK LOOK _____

Session Topic   Walking in the Holy Spirit is the dynamic of a changed life.

Session Goals   You will help group members:
1. Take the first step on the road to a changed life (*Focus*).
2. Be made aware of the steps by which life is changed (*Discover*).
3. Resolve to walk in the Spirit (*Respond*).

GETTING READY _____

What You'll Need

Bible
Be Dynamic
MTM-7
Overhead projector
Chalkboard and chalk

Getting Ready to Teach

1. Study chapter 10 of *Be Dynamic* and read Acts 9:32–10:48.
2. Continue your log of "Accidentals and Essentials."
3. Prepare an overhead transparency of MTM-7.

THE LESSON _____

=================== FOCUS ===================

1. Begin this session by sharing your life purpose statement. Then ask group members to share theirs. This time of sharing should be to the point, with very little commenting. Following this time of sharing, select several

persons to lead in a prayer of commitment. Conclude this activity by singing a song of commitment, such as "I Have Decided to Follow Jesus" or "I Am Resolved No Longer to Linger."

2. Point out that a changed life begins with one step. Explain that the formulation of a life purpose statement is a first step. But if it is to have meaning it must be followed with other steps. In this session Peter testifies to the reality of a changed life brought about by many *changes* or steps.

DISCOVER

1. Review your log of "Accidentals and Essentials" with your group. Note especially Dr. Wiersbe's comments about these distinctions in this session. Ask group members to classify the three miracles of this lesson.

2. Ask group members to locate the four acts of "the greatest miracle": winning lost sinners. List them on the chalkboard and discuss each in turn.

As "Preparation" is discussed, help your group see that the preparation was two-sided. God not only prepared Peter, but He also prepared Cornelius. Read Dr. Wiersbe's comments on the seeking Saviour finding the seeking sinner. Point out that the events surrounding the conversion of Cornelius relate to the most often-asked questions: Are the heathen lost? Are people who have never heard of Christ condemned? Read John 3:18 and point out that personal faith in Jesus is essential for salvation. Then read John 3:16-17 and point out that there is another side—God loves sinners. That love is seen in God bringing Peter to Cornelius. Explain that God knows the hearts of men and moves directly or through circumstances to bring a seeking sinner into contact with the Gospel. Ask: **What other example of God directly bringing a seeking sinner into contact with the Gospel have we studied?** (the Ethiopian eunuch) **What example is there in Acts that shows God using circumstances to bring sinners and believers together?** (Samaritans through the circumstance of persecution, Acts 8:4-5.) Amplify this idea by noting that many times we hear missionaries speaking of a call or a burden for a particular country or tribe. Explain that this is evidence of God's Spirit directing Christians to seeking sinners. Have group members suggest ways in which this relates to them.

In the discussion of "Explanation," read Dr. Wiersbe's comments on Peter's question. Ask if there are other possible reasons for Peter's question. One possibility is that Peter was using a question in the same manner that Jesus did with Saul in Acts 9:4—not to gain information, but to heighten Cornelius' awareness of his own motives.

3. Using MTM-7, discuss the steps in Peter's experience that led to a changed life. Begin by pointing out that the term changed life is commonly used, but the term changing life more accurately describes the Christian life. Peter's life changed as he walked in the Spirit.

Use some of the following ideas to develop this principle:

☐ *Step 1.* The Word of God is our primary resource in knowing God's will. If this step is not taken, then no further steps can be taken.

☐ *Step 2.* Peter was filled; he was surrendered to the Holy Spirit.

☐ *Step 3.* Peter was not ashamed of Christ before men.

☐ *Step 4.* Peter had to make a critical choice. His decision to obey God *rather* than man severed his loyalty to Judaism.

☐ *Step 5.* No reservations are noted; perhaps his association with Jesus among the Samaritans helped him overcome his prejudice (John 4:1-43; Luke 17:11-19).

☐ *Steps 6–9.* Discuss Dr. Wiersbe's remarks on these events.

☐ *Step 10.* This acceptance was twofold. In verses 25-26 he elevates Cornelius to his level. In verse 28 he lowers himself to Cornelius' level.

☐ *Step 11.* In this act of baptism, Cornelius publicly identified himself with Christ. But in baptizing, Peter publicly identified himself with the Gentiles. This was not a secret ceremony, and Peter would have to offer a defense for his action (Acts 11:1-18).

Draw attention to the fact that these changes in Peter's life took place over a 10-year period.

RESPOND

1. Illustrate how we have difficulty with time today. We have instant coffee, we have microwaves, we have instant credit. Sometimes we carry this over into our Christian lives. We want instant spiritual maturity. We become impatient with the apparent slowness of the Spirit of God.

2. Remind your group of the first step taken in a life purpose statement. Explain that it is *only* a step. Encourage them to maintain their relationship with God by walking in the Spirit. Remind them that a changed life is the result of a *changing* life.

ASSIGNMENT

1. Have group members study chapter 11 of *Be Dynamic* and Acts 11.

2. Have group members continue logging "Accidentals and Essentials."

3. Ask a group member to prepare a report on the Gentile assistance to the Jerusalem church. Tell him or her to read Acts 11:27-30; Romans 15:25-28; 1 Corinthians 16:1-4; 2 Corinthians 8–9 and answer these questions: What motivated the Gentiles to give? What obligated their giving? What guidelines were given to them? How did God's grace affect them?

Making Room for the Gentiles

TEXT, CHAPTER 11

A QUICK LOOK

Session Topic   Love is the dynamic of Christian unity.

Session Goals   You will help group members:
1. Identify biblical love by its practical dynamic (*Focus*).
2. Explore the dynamic of love in bringing about one church (*Discover*).
3. List ways in which they can express their love for others (*Respond*).

GETTING READY

*What
You'll Need*   Bible
Be Dynamic
Chalkboard and chalk

*Getting Ready
to Teach*
1. Study chapter 11 of *Be Dynamic* and Acts 11.
2. Continue your log of "Accidentals and Essentials."
3. Check with the person who accepted the assignment on Gentile assistance and offer help if needed.

THE LESSON

=========================== FOCUS ===========================

Lead the group in a discussion of love. Ask: **What are the differences between the world's concept of love and the biblical concept of love?** Point out that biblical love is never ambiguous or theoretical. It is vital, active, and vigorous. It indeed has hands, feet, eyes, and ears. In this session love is shown to be the dynamic which overthrew human barriers and established the unity of the body of Christ.

1. Review group members' logs of "Accidentals and Essentials." Relate to the discussion, Dr. Wiersbe's remarks under, "They Accepted the Gentiles."

2. Discuss the issue raised in the Jewish Christian community. Ask: **What criticism was raised against Peter?** (Peter ate with Gentiles.) Explain that eating with someone in that society was tantamount to making a commitment or a covenant. To eat together implied mutual obligations to each other for peace and protection. To take advantage of someone you had eaten with was an offense of the first magnitude. The Jew thought himself violated if he in any way placed himself under obligation to a Gentile. Amplify this by reminding your group of the seriousness of violating the Lord's Table (1 Corinthians 11:27-32).

Explain that as Peter justified his behavior the Jews began to understand that culture (tradition) was secondary to God's principles. Have someone read Mark 7:1-13. Explain that the problem is made clear by Jesus. The Jews constantly held customs above and therefore contrary to the Law. They were doing the same thing in regard to eating with Gentiles. Ask: **What customs could a Jew continue to observe as a Christian? What customs would be wrong? What customs of our society are wrong for Christians? What customs do not necessarily conflict with God's will?**

Discuss the matter of legalism as a motivation for the Christian life. Ask: **What are the signs of a legalistic church or Christian? What attitudes are fostered by a legalistic outlook?** Point out that love is the proper Christian motivation. Have someone read 1 Corinthians 13. Discuss how love overcomes customs through a concern for the individual himself.

3. Explain that Barnabas exemplifies the love that overlooks incidentals and brings unity to the believing community. Ask: **What does the name Barnabas mean?** (Son of encouragement) **What two things did Barnabas previously do to encourage believers?** (Sold property and contributed the proceeds to the church. Encouraged the Jerusalem believers to accept Saul.) **Why do you think Barnabas was chosen to investigate the reports of Antioch?** (Most likely the Jerusalem church wanted to encourage the church at Antioch.) **What ways did Barnabas encourage the church at Antioch?** (He was glad for them; he exhorted them.) **In what ways was Barnabas an encouragement by his own testimony?** (He was a good man, spiritual, and faithful.) **When Barnabas brought Saul to Antioch, who do you think he was trying to encourage?** (Both Saul and the church.) Point out that encouragement is more often than not mutual to all involved. Ask: **In what ways did this encouragement serve all parties?** As you discuss this, don't forget Barnabas as one of the parties. Point out that Barnabas was selected to bring relief back to Jerusalem from Antioch. Thus the encouragement from the Jerusalem church prompted encouragement from the Antioch Christians.

4. Explain that the drought along with its effects took its toll on the church in Jerusalem for many years. The response of the Gentile believers in Antioch was the first of many relief shipments to Jerusalem. Eventually relief came from the churches in Rome, Corinth, Berea, Thessalonica, Philippi, and many others. Ask the person who was assigned to report on this Gentile assistance to share his or her findings with the group. If overlooked, point out that the drought affected not only Jerusalem but the rest of the world (v. 28). Thus it may have been responsible for the deep poverty of the church of Macedonia as well. Discuss "giving" as a basic manifestation of love.

5. Dr. Wiersbe points out the developing organization of the early church. As this is discussed, amplify this by explaining that the church is both an organism and an organization. Write these terms side by side on the chalkboard. Then ask group members to offer examples of each. List them under the appropriate heading. Some examples are:

ORGANISM	ORGANIZATION
the church is a body	the church has officers
the church is indwelt by the Spirit	the church has ordinances

Discuss the relationship of love to each attribute.

RESPOND

Distribute paper and pencils and have group members list ways and means to be an encouragement to others. Remind them that encouragement comes in many forms: personal concern, words of comfort and understanding, deeds, and gifts to meet a special need. Ask group members to prepare a list of specific ways in which they can show their love and concern for specific individuals. Instruct them to use this form: "**I will encourage** _____ **by** _____." Illustrate on the chalkboard with the following example: "**I will encourage my wife by telling her, 'I love you.'**"

ASSIGNMENT

1. Have group members study chapter 12 of *Be Dynamic* and Acts 12.
2. Have group members conclude their logs of "Accidentals and Essentials."
3. If possible, arrange to take your group on a field trip to a local power plant. This will make next session's Focus more significant. This would be a good opportunity for fellowship outside of the study group.

Wake Up to a Miracle!

TEXT, CHAPTER 12

A QUICK LOOK _____

Session Topic   Prayer is the dynamic of Christian accomplishment.

Session Goals   You will help group members:
1. Compare the dynamic of prayer to the dynamos of electricity (*Focus*).
2. Discover the importance of prayer in the life of the church (*Discover*).
3. Begin a regular system of praying as a group (*Respond*).

GETTING READY _____

What You'll Need
Bible
Be Dynamic
MTM-8
Overhead projector
Chalkboard and chalk
A copy of *Fox's Book of Martyrs*, edited by W.B. Forbush

Getting Ready to Teach
1. Study chapter 12 of *Be Dynamic* and Acts 12.
2. Conclude your log of the "Accidentals and Essentials" in Acts.
3. Using your concordance, make a study of answered prayer in the Bible.
4. If desired, add further information about the apostles' deaths from *Fox's Book of Martyrs*.
5. If possible, take your group on a visit to a power station.

THE LESSON

FOCUS

Adapt the following to your needs, depending on whether or not your group was able to visit a power station.

Display MTM-8 with the lower half covered. Point to each room in the house and ask: **What electrical units or appliances are shown? What other possible electric units may be found in this room?** As this progresses, it will become apparent that electrical power is a major part of our life today.

Ask: **Where does the electricity come from?** (From the outlets, from power lines, but ultimately from the power station.) Uncover the lower half of the MTM and explain that, whether we know it or not, the electrical energy in our homes comes from turbines or dynamos. Remind your group that we seldom, if ever, think about the source of our power.

Inform group members that in this session you will be studying the source of the church's power, and like electricity, it is seldom considered. Peter's electrifying miracle of deliverance is the first scene. Then the power source is revealed—the church at prayer.

DISCOVER

1. Review of your log of "Accidentals and Essentials."

2. James, the son of Zebedee, the brother of John, was the first apostle to be martyred. Share the following rundown of the other apostles' place and manner of death according to tradition:

☐ Peter was crucified at Rome (see John 21:18-19).

☐ John died peaceably at Ephesus (the only apostle to escape martyrdom).

☐ Andrew was crucified at Edessa.

☐ Philip was crucified in Phrygia.

☐ Thomas was speared to death in India.

☐ Bartholomew was crucified in India.

☐ Matthew was slain with a halberd in Ethiopia.

☐ James, son of Alphaeus, was stoned at Jerusalem.

☐ Simon Zelotes was crucified in Britain.

☐ Jude (Thaddeus) was crucified at Edessa.

☐ Matthias was stoned at Jerusalem.

3. The circumstances of James and Peter emphasize the interplay between the sovereign will of God and prayer. Point out that this sometimes is difficult to reconcile. Ask: **What is the danger of exaggerating the sovereign will of God?** (Fatalism; God will do what He wants whether I pray or not.) **How can the two be reconciled?** (By praying in God's will or being willing to accept His will.) **Why can we have confidence in prayer?** (Because God commands us to pray. It is His *will* that we pray.) Point out that God

governs His universe by certain fixed laws. Prayer is one of these laws. God has designed to bring many things about through prayer. Help group members to see that refusing to pray is a sin.

4. In Acts 12:5, mention is made of prayer without ceasing. Have several persons read Romans 1:9; 1 Thessalonians 1:3; 2:13; 5:17. Ask: **What could it mean to pray without ceasing?** (To pray every waking minute, to be in an attitude of prayer, to pray regularly until an answer is received.) **Which is the most likely meaning?** (To pray regularly until an answer is received.) Help your group see that this is actually what the church was doing in Acts 12.

5. Dr. Wiersbe attributes the church's response to Peter's appearance as an element of unbelief. This is certainly a real possibility. You may want to suggest another possibility. The surprise of the church may be due to the manner of Peter's release. They may have been expecting Peter to be released through normal channels rather than by a miracle. Either way an element of unbelief may be present. Discuss the problem of unbelief in prayer. Ask: **Why do we often pray without complete faith? How does this affect answers to our prayers? Why does God respond to our prayers when there is an element of unbelief? How can we develop our faith in prayer? Do you think the church's prayer life was different after Peter's release? In what ways?**

6. Write on the chalkboard Dr. Wiersbe's comment, "Instead of Peter being killed by Herod, it was Herod who was killed by Peter's God!" Emphasize the lesson in this passage that God always has the last word. Here again is the balance of God's sovereignty and man's responsibility. Ask someone to read Ephesians 3:20. The church prayed for Peter's deliverance and God answered that prayer *and* more. He also delivered Herod—to judgment.

7. Read from the text the paragraph that begins, "The early church had no 'political clout'..." Ask someone to read 1 Timothy 2:1-3. Discuss the relationship of prayer and politics. Ask: **What steps are Christians today taking in the affairs of our nation?** (Running for political office, demonstrations, write-in campaigns, etc.) Draw attention to the fact that God's order is first of all, to pray. Point out that as good as many of these activities are, they cannot take precedence over prayer. Nor can they be a substitute for prayer. Discuss the possibility that the church's lack of influence in our nation may be directly related to a lack of prayer.

================= RESPOND =================

Have group members suggest ways in which they can as a group be involved in prayer. (These may include: meeting before or after the session for prayer, a telephone prayer chain in times of urgency, or a prayer breakfast.) Challenge your group to select those which best fit your situation, and begin regular prayer together.

1. Have group members read through Acts 1–12.

2. Have group members make a list of things which have been studied in this session which they would like to review or discuss more fully.

3. Ask group members to come to the next session prepared to share what they have most benefited from in this study.

Review

TEXT, CHAPTER 13

A QUICK LOOK

Session Topic   The dynamics of the church of Acts are the same dynamics of the church today.

Session Goals   You will help group members:
1. Share the benefits that they received in this study (*Focus*).
2. Review the basic concepts that made the church in Acts dynamic (*Discover*).
3. Resolve to continue the commitments made during this study (*Respond*).

GETTING READY

What You'll Need

Bible
Be Dynamic
Selected MTMs
Overhead projector
Chalkboard and chalk

Getting Ready to Teach

1. Read Acts 1–12. Note anything that you have not seen previously.
2. Read *Be Dynamic* and make notes of points you may have missed.
3. Select MTMs that you will want to use in this review.

THE LESSON

===== FOCUS =====

Begin this session with testimonies from group members on the subject:

Benefits I have received from this study of Acts 1–12. Be sure to give your testimony as well.

===================== DISCOVER =====================

1. Ask group members if they have something relating to Acts 1–12 that they would like to review or discuss more fully.

2. Review Acts 1–12 from the perspective of Acts 1:8. Remind group members that this is the key verse. Ask: **What four themes of Acts are given in this verse?** (The geographical growth of the church, the Holy Spirit, power or dynamic, and witness.) Briefly trace these four themes through Acts 1–12.

3. Review with the group Peter's use of the keys of the kingdom. This is important in understanding Matthew 16:18-19 and Peter's activity in the Book of Acts. Be sure group members comprehend the relationship of Christ's prophecy and Peter's fulfillment of it.

4. Ask group members to list the major persons of Acts 1–2. Write them on the chalkboard as given. Ask group members to give a short biographical sketch of each.

5. The regular use of a log of "Accidentals and Essentials" has been encouraged throughout this study. Determine its effectiveness in helping your group members understand the transitory elements of Acts 1–12. If desired, review some of the more salient events to make sure that this principle is understood.

6. On the chalkboard, list the dynamic suggested for each session. Discuss these as they relate to the church today. As each dynamic is discussed, remind your group that Dr. Wiersbe's book is entitled *Be Dynamic*, not *Was Dynamic*.

===================== RESPOND =====================

1. Review with your group the projects that were begun during the course of this study (see Respond section in sessions 4, 7, 9, 11, and 12). Ask group members to evaluate their progress in each.

2. Challenge group members to continue in those commitments which they have made; to continue to grow through new commitments; and above all, to **Be Dynamic!**